Harry's Goldfield Adventure

By Dee White
Illustrated by Rachel Tonkin

Contents

Chapter 1

Harry Takes a Fall

HARRY OPENED THE CREAKY DOOR to the old shearing shed. The wind howled through the tin walls. Harry didn't like going into the spooky old shed. But today he had to.

"Here, Charlie. Here, puss, puss, puss. Aunt Linda says you have to come inside. It's dinner time."

Harry heard a miaow. He looked up. Charlie was sitting on one of the old rafters. He looked down at Harry as if to say, "Come up and get me."

Harry was staying with his Aunt Linda on her farm for the school holidays. He loved Aunt Linda's stories about the old farm and how it had been built on an old gold-mining site.

But right now, Harry was more interested in getting Charlie down from the rafters. "Come on, Charlie." Harry was getting hungry himself.

Charlie just started cleaning his fur.

In the corner of the shearing shed was an old stepladder. It was heavy, but Harry managed to drag it across the wooden floor until he was just under the cat.

"I'll have to get you down myself," he grumbled as he opened the ladder.

As he climbed onto the first rung, there was a loud creaking noise. Suddenly, the floor beneath the ladder gave way.

"Help!" Harry shouted as he fell . . . down . . . down . . . into darkness.

Harry tried to open his eyes. Everything was blurry. It felt like he was lying on the ground. He opened his eyes wider.

Where am I? he thought. *And where is that light coming from?*

He lifted his head. He seemed to be in a dimly lit tunnel. Was he at the bottom of the shearing shed? Harry had no idea.

Just then, he heard a noise. He turned his head quickly and saw a man holding a lantern. The man wore long pants, an open blue shirt with a striped top underneath and a wide-brimmed hat.

The strangest part about his outfit was the handkerchief he wore around his neck. The man had a dark, bushy beard. Harry thought he looked like a pirate.

But even though the man looked wild, his eyes were friendly when he smiled at Harry.

"Was that you I heard, lad?" the man asked Harry. "Did you fall down the shaft—are you all right?"

Harry stood up slowly. "What are you doing in Aunt Linda's shed?" he croaked.

The man looked puzzled. "Aunt Linda's shed? What are you talking about?"

"Who are you?" asked Harry.

The man held out his hand. "My name's William Brown, but my friends call me Bill. And who might you be, lad?"

Hesitantly, Harry placed his hand in Bill's large, rough-looking one. "I'm Harry."

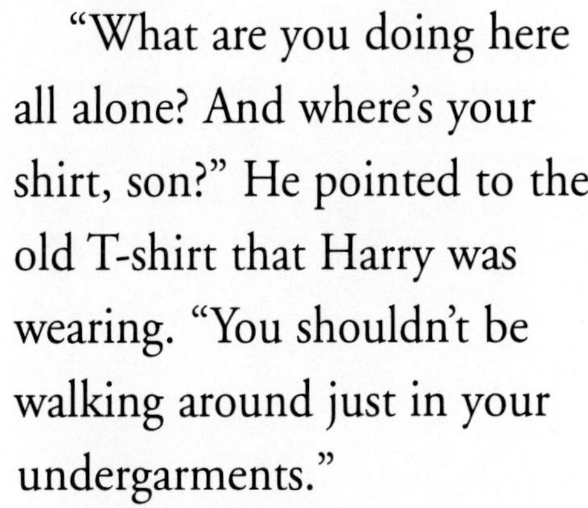

"What are you doing here all alone? And where's your shirt, son?" He pointed to the old T-shirt that Harry was wearing. "You shouldn't be walking around just in your undergarments."

Harry shook his head, confused. What did Bill mean? What was wrong with his T-shirt? And where was he if he wasn't on Aunt Linda's farm?

"I… I don't know," he said. He felt tears prick in the corner of his eyes.

Bill looked at him kindly. "Never mind, lad. Come back to the camp with me. You can borrow one of my shirts."

Harry blinked back his tears. He didn't know what else to do, so he followed Bill along the tunnel. They climbed up some steep stairs that had been carved into the earth and headed towards the daylight.

Chapter 2

A Trip to Town

AS THEY CAME OUT INTO THE SUN, Harry looked around. Where was Aunt Linda's farm?

Everything looked different. There were tents everywhere, but they didn't look like any of the tents Harry had ever camped in. They were just pieces of canvas draped over tree branches.

Bill stopped in front of one of the tents. Like all the others, it didn't even have a front.

"How do you keep the flies out?" asked Harry.

Bill laughed. "If that's the only thing that comes into your tent, you can consider yourself lucky." He ducked inside and started looking for something.

"What else comes in?" asked Harry. He didn't like some of the noises that he was hearing from the nearby bushes.

"Don't worry, lad. Nothing I can't take care of," said Bill's voice from inside the tent.

He came out and handed Harry a shirt. "Put this on, then we'd better keep going."

"Where?" asked Harry as he put on the shirt.

"Becky James, the Gold Commissioner's daughter, has gone missing, and I'm looking for her. I was on my way into town when I heard you down in the mine."

Harry followed Bill into the town. It didn't look like any town he knew of. The shops were small wooden huts, all standing close together. They had low roofs made of thick bark pieces, little windows and crooked doors.

Bill and Harry went into some of the shops to ask if anyone had seen Becky. The butcher hadn't seen her. Neither had Mrs Grey, the owner of the general store. "I hope she hasn't fallen down a mine shaft, poor girl," she said.

Harry nodded. He knew what that felt like.

"She can't be down a shaft—one of the miners would have seen her," said Bill.

They looked in a barber's shop window, where a man was having his beard trimmed with a sharp-looking knife.

"Sorry, I haven't seen little Becky," said the barber. "Hope you find her before it gets dark, poor little mite."

The next shop they walked into was the baker's. The smell of fresh bread baking made Harry's stomach rumble.

Across the road from the bakery was the printer's shop where they made the newspaper. Harry thought it might give him a clue about where he was. "Can we go in there?"

Bill frowned. "We'll need to make it quick. Stay well clear of that printing press. It could rip your arm off."

"I'll be careful," said Harry.

The newspaper was called *The Morning Star*. As they walked through the door, Harry made sure that he kept as far away as he could from the loud, clunking printing press.

"We're looking for Becky James. Have you seen her?" Bill yelled to the man behind the counter who was carefully folding maps.

Harry picked up a copy of *The Morning Star* and read aloud, "Tuesday, 20th December, 1859. Why does it say that?"

Bill seemed surprised by the question. "That's today's date, lad."

Chapter 3

Back in Time

HARRY COULDN'T BELIEVE IT. When he woke up at Aunt Linda's this morning, it was 20 December 2009. Somehow, he had gone back in time—150 years.

This was the scariest yet most exciting thing that had ever happened to him!

"You know, Harry, you remind me of someone who is very dear to my heart," Bill said as they walked out of the printer's shop.

He stopped and pulled a piece of paper out of his pocket. On it was a drawing of a girl about Harry's age.

"That's my daughter, Nellie. I came here from England to find gold—and a better life for my family."

Harry looked around. "Life doesn't seem that easy here."

Bill closed his eyes and breathed deeply. "At least the air's fresh."

Harry looked at the picture of the girl. "She looks a lot like me."

Bill smiled. "So she does. I drew it myself."

"It's a great picture," said Harry. "I wish I could draw like that."

"Drawing is the only thing that keeps me sane in this place," said Bill. He looked sad. "I miss Nellie, you know—and my wife, Colleen."

"So, what else do you do around here, when you're not down the mines?" asked Harry.

"Mostly sit around the camp fire and tell stories, and sing and play music."

Harry scratched his head. "What do you play music on?"

"Well, Leo plays a merry tune on his fiddle, and there's Dave, on his flute."

"Do you play an instrument?"

Bill shook his head. "No, but I love to sing."

Harry wanted to know more about this man and his strange world. "Have you found much gold?"

Bill shook his head. "No, and most of my money has gone towards food and paying for my miner's licence."

"Miner's licence?" Harry was surprised. "You have to pay to mine?"

Bill nodded. "It used to be a lot worse. We used to have to pay to renew our miner's licence every month—even if we hadn't found gold."

"That's so unfair!" said Harry. "How long have you been here?"

"Three years."

Harry thought about his own home. He wondered when or if he would ever get back there.

"When are you going back to England?" he asked Bill.

Bill snorted. "Don't plan to. No work, no future back there."

"But what about your family?"

Bill bowed his head. "I'd bring them over here if I had the money."

Harry suddenly remembered that this morning Aunt Linda had given him pocket money for doing jobs around the farm. He put his hand in his pocket and pulled out his five-dollar note. He handed it to Bill. "Maybe this will help."

"What's that?"

"Money."

"I can't take your money, lad. Besides, I'd get arrested if I tried to use notes that weren't made on these goldfields.

"There's no money like that around here. But thanks to you anyway."

Harry tucked the five-dollar note back in his jeans. "How will you get the money, then, to bring your family over?"

"The Commissioner has offered a reward to the person who finds his little girl. That would set me up nicely."

"I hope we find her." Harry didn't like to think of anyone lost out here—and he wanted Bill to be with his family again.

Bill grinned. "Me too! Wouldn't that be grand?"

"Do you know how much the reward will be?" asked Harry.

"Enough to pay for my wife, Colleen, and Nellie to come over from England by ship."

Harry screwed up his nose in surprise. "Ship? Why don't they come by plane? It would be heaps quicker."

It was Bill's turn to look surprised. "What's a plane?"

Harry drew a picture in the mud using a small stick. He drew the wings and the body of a plane.

Bill nodded. "Ah, a type of bird, is it?"

Harry drew wheels on the plane.

Bill laughed. "Now I know you're joking! Never seen a bird with wheels."

Harry suddenly thought that planes probably hadn't even been invented yet. "Never mind," he said quickly.

Chapter 4

Camping Out

"**NO SIGN OF BECKY** around town. And it's getting dark," said Bill. "Time to head back to camp."

Bill shared a tent with two other miners, the musicians Dave and Leo.

"Harry's staying for a while," Bill told the men.

"Fine with us," said Dave. "As long as we have grub and somewhere to sleep, we don't mind sharing."

They sat around the huge camp fire to keep warm. Bill cooked mutton and made some flat bread he called "damper".

Afterwards, Harry was feeling full, and warm from the camp fire. His eyelids started to droop and his head began to nod.

"Bedtime, lad," said Bill. "You can have my bed. I'll be fine on the ground."

"Thanks, Bill," Harry said sleepily. "I hope we find Becky tomorrow."

Bill's bed was an old hessian bag tied up between four tree stumps. There was not much of a pillow, and there were no blankets. It didn't look very comfortable, but Harry was so tired he didn't care.

Harry lay down on the bed and closed his eyes. He thought he'd fall asleep immediately, but his mind started racing.

His first thoughts were of home. Aunt Linda would be worried sick by now. Harry needed to find a way to get back to his own time. But he couldn't leave—not yet. Bill had been so kind to him, and he needed Harry's help.

If Harry and Bill could find Becky, then Bill could use the reward money to bring Nellie and her mother to Australia, and Bill could be with his family again.

After Harry helped Bill, he could go home—if only he could work out how to get back.

Then Harry thought of Becky, who wasn't sleeping in her own bed tonight either. It would be awful to be alone out there. Harry wondered if Becky was hiding or if she was stuck somewhere and couldn't get out. At home, Harry played hide-and-seek in the garage, but nobody here had a garage—they didn't even have cars.

When Harry finally fell asleep, he dreamed about Aunt Linda's farm. He dreamed he was climbing up the ladder in the shearing shed to get Charlie.

Then he was falling, falling, falling into the bottom of the mine shaft again.

But this time he heard a little girl sobbing. "Becky?" he called into the blackness. "Becky, is that you?"

Chapter 5

Back Down the Shaft

HARRY WOKE with a start. His heart was thumping. Suddenly, he knew where Becky was. Bill was snoring on the ground. Harry leaned over the bed and shook him by the shoulder.

"What?" said Bill, waking up. "What's going on?"

"I know where Becky is. I dreamed about her."

Bill sat up. "You did?"

Harry nodded. "I think she might have fallen down a mine shaft."

"She can't have. One of the miners would have found her when they went to work." Bill sighed.

Suddenly, Bill was on his feet. "But Bob Harris and Jamie Turner didn't work yesterday! They got hurt in a fight at the hotel the day before. Becky could have fallen down their shaft."

"I'm coming with you," Harry said. "I can show you where she is from my dream. I heard a little girl crying and, in my head, I saw her down the mine shaft."

Bill frowned, then nodded. "All right. But stay close, lad." With Bill in the lead, they walked through the camp and carefully around the open mine shafts.

Then Bill stopped. "This is it," he said. "Becky! Becky!" he called down into the shaft. There was no answer.

"I hope she's okay," said Harry. "Maybe she can't hear us—it's a long way down there."

Suddenly, Harry heard something… a faint voice, calling back. "Did you hear that, Bill? Listen!"

Bill climbed down the shaft first, lighting the way with a lantern.

The ladder was steep and Harry nearly lost his balance several times. He was worried. Becky had fallen a long way. He hoped she wasn't badly hurt.

Suddenly, they heard her again. "I'm down here." Becky's tearful voice drifted up to them.

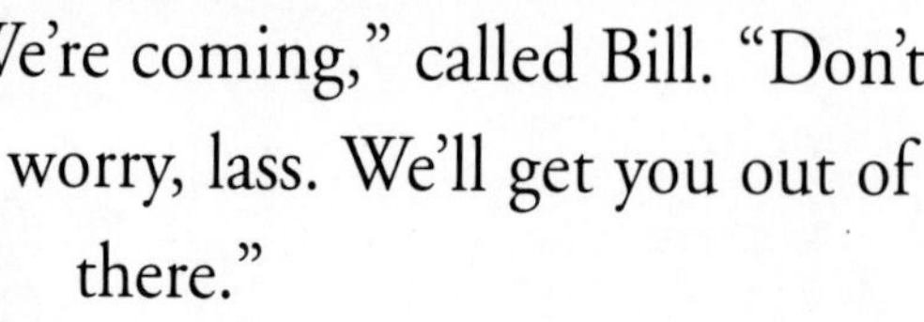

"We're coming," called Bill. "Don't worry, lass. We'll get you out of there."

They climbed faster.

Finally, they reached the bottom and there was Becky. She was sitting on the floor of the mine, sobbing. Dark curls bounced around her tear-stained face. She wore a baggy pinafore that reached down to the top of her black lace-up boots.

"My ankle hurts," she moaned.

"You'll be fine, lass. We'll have you out of here soon," said Bill.

With Harry's help, Bill carefully lifted Becky onto his back.

Slowly, they made their way back up the ladder into daylight.

Commissioner James and his wife were overjoyed to see their daughter. The Commissioner carried Becky to a chair and put another chair in front of her. "Here, darling, rest your leg on this," he said.

"I don't think her ankle's broken, but it looks sore," said Bill.

While Mrs James comforted her daughter and bandaged her ankle, the Commissioner thanked Bill and Harry.

"We're so grateful to you both."

"Harry's the one who found her," said Bill.

The Commissioner handed a bundle of notes to Bill. "You two certainly earned this reward."

"Thank you. I just kept thinking of my own daughter, Nellie, and I knew I had to do my best to find your Becky," said Bill.

Mrs James called them over, "Mr Brown, Harry, you must both stay for lunch. I insist."

"We won't say no to that, Mrs James," replied Bill. "Thank you kindly."

After lunch, Bill and Harry went back to the camp to count the reward money. Dave came over with *The Morning Star* newspaper.

"You two will be on the front page tomorrow," he said, giving the newspaper to Harry.

While Bill finished counting the money, Harry read *The Morning Star*. "Oh no!" he said.

"What's wrong?" Bill asked.

"It says that with all the miners bringing their families over, the price of a boat ticket is a lot more than it was this time last year."

"Oh, no!" Bill slumped miserably.

“The reward money won’t be enough.”

“Don’t worry, mate,” said Dave. “We’ll think of something.”

There must be something I can do, thought Harry. If only he could find gold—then he could sell it and give the money to his friend. *I know how to pan for gold*, he thought. *Maybe I should try that.*

While Bill and Dave talked about the newspaper article, Harry grabbed Bill’s heavy metal pan and crept out of the tent.

He had been panning for gold with his Aunt Linda many times before. *I know just the place to look*, Harry thought.

He hurried towards the river.

Chapter 6

Harry's Gold

A RIVER RAN along the far boundary of Aunt Linda's farm. Harry and his aunt had spent many warm spring days panning there and having picnics next to the water.

"This river used to be full of gold," Aunt Linda had told Harry.

She had shown him how to use the water to separate the gold flakes from the river sand and pebbles.

Harry was glad to get to the river. Bill's pan was heavy and Harry was keen to start looking for gold.

There were lots of people in and around the water—including a boy about Harry's age and a younger girl.

"Are you new here?" asked the girl.

Harry nodded.

"I'm Beth and this is Sam. You can pan with us if you like."

"Thanks." Harry knelt down next to them and lowered his pan into the water.

They swished the stones and water around the pans to separate them. They pulled out each stone and checked it for gold before tossing it back in the water.

Harry filled his pan with stones and sand from the river. It was so heavy he could hardly swish the water around.

He was just about to tip it all out in frustration when Sam yelled, "Wait! I think I saw something sparkle."

Bit by bit, they emptied the pan. At the bottom were two sparkling rocks. They were as big as marbles.

"Beth, come and look," yelled Sam. "Harry found gold!"

Aunt Linda had only ever found tiny flakes of gold. Harry couldn't believe they had found such big pieces.

Beth held them up towards the sunlight to get a better look. Then she started jumping up and down with excitement. "These will be worth a lot. I wish we could find some like that. We'd be rich!"

Harry handed one of the rocks to Sam. "This is yours," he said. "We were panning together."

"Thanks!" Sam grinned, clutching the gold tightly.

Harry ran back to Bill's tent as fast as he could.

"Look what I found, Bill!" said Harry, grinning broadly. He held out the gold.

"Gold!" said Bill. "You're rich!"

Harry handed the rock to Bill. "Now you'll have enough money to bring your family over," he said.

"I can't take this."

"Of course you can, Bill. You need it more than me," said Harry.

Chapter 7

Going Home

"WELL, THEN YOU have to take this, Harry." Bill handed Harry the drawing of Nellie. "Most valuable thing I own," he said.

"But don't you need it?"

Bill tapped his head. "Memory's up here," he said. "And soon I'll have the real Nellie with me. I want you to have it—to remember me, and what a good thing you did."

After Bill left for the bank to get the gold weighed, Harry thought about Becky, and how she was safely back with her family. Once Nellie and Colleen were here, Harry would be the only one who wasn't where he belonged.

He wandered across to the mine shaft where they'd found Becky. It was right next to the mine shaft he'd arrived in. He sat down. The afternoon sun was warm on his shoulders. He slipped off Bill's shirt and lay back with his hands behind his head.

"Wake up, sleepy," said a voice. It was Sam, and he had a huge clump of dirt in his hand, ready to throw it.

Harry dived to his right. The soil next to the shaft was loose. He felt it sliding underneath him. Harry tried to roll across to solid ground, but he wasn't quick enough. He felt himself slipping.

The last thing he remembered as he fell into darkness was Sam's scared face.

"You're awake!"

Harry wasn't sure where he was for a second. Then he realised he was in his bed at Aunt Linda's farm—and Charlie was next to him, purring. Harry's back was sore. He wondered if it was from sleeping in Bill's bed, or falling down the mine shaft—twice.

"My back hurts, and my ankle," said Harry.

"You've sprained it. You'll be a bit sore for a while, but you were very lucky," said Aunt Linda.

Harry smiled.

Aunt Linda hugged him. "I'm *so* sorry, Harry. I didn't know that old mine shaft was under the shed. I've had it covered over properly now."

Aunt Linda left the room to get Harry some water. Harry closed his eyes. He wondered whether Bill, Becky and the miners had just been a dream. Then he remembered something…

Slowly, he reached into the pocket of his jeans, and carefully pulled out the piece of paper. He unfolded it and grinned as he looked at Bill's drawing of his little girl.

Aunt Linda came back in with a glass of water. "What's this?" She picked up the piece of paper. "Harry, where on earth did you get this picture of your Great-Great-Aunt Nellie?"

Harry smiled as he took the paper from her, and held it tightly to his chest.

A Glossary of Goldfield Words

canvas a type of heavy material that is used to make tents

damper a type of bread made from flour and water that is cooked over a camp fire

fiddle violin

Gold Commissioner the person in charge of a gold mining site, who checked miners' licences and settled arguments between miners

hessian a type of strong material that is used to make sacks

miner's licence a licence that miners had to buy from the government if they wanted to dig for gold

mutton a type of meat from a well-grown or adult sheep, older than lamb

panning a way of finding gold in a riverbed. You use a large pan-shaped dish and water to separate the riverbed sand from the gold.

pinafore a loose dress that girls wore over their other clothes, like an apron

printing press a machine used to print newspapers and books

rafters the beams that support the roof

rickety shaky; not very sturdy

shaft a long sloping passage that goes down under the ground to a mine